"There was a door

to which I found no key

There was a veil past

which I could not see

Some little talk a while

of me and thee

And then there seem'd –

no more of thee and me"

From Taman Shu
in The Rubaiyat of Omar Khayyam

Buttermere sunset

Buttermere Return

Claire Griffel

Dedicated to

David Griffel

and

Idrissa Sané

Claire Griffel's first word was "No" and she hasn't
stopped talking and telling tales since.
when she learned to walk her first steps
were sideways ... all possibly a sign of things to come.

Imagine Senegal 2021

With my thanks to

The Richardsons of Buttermere

Elizabeth Coulthard
Wendy Storer
Alison Crane nee White
Celia Cartwright
Cylla Cole
Annette Wood
Debbie Nicholas
Jim Farish
Matthew Connolly
Jackie Gaskell
Mat Butler
Natasha Kröger-Wyllie
Megan Robinson

The Mckenzie family at Wood House

With thanks of remembrance to Eva Erdéyli nee Neuburg

And everyone who has believed in me

The doors of Gatesgarth Farm under Fleetwith Pike were opened wide

by the Richardson family to let my Father in.

This is how Buttermere became a refuge.

This is how we,

as a family, came to Buttermere.

My two brothers came with Father.

My Mother came with him.

I came for the first time as a sparkle in my Mother's eyes.

Eventually we even brought the cat.

Gatesgarth

My Brother David, Mother Dorothy, me, my Father Wladimir and Marmaduke the marmalade cat

1

For fifty years I was part of valley life. After the first day of May in 2009 I did not return for a decade. Was it a choice? I left behind

two people who were for me a Grandfather and a Grandmother. I left behind my Father, my Mother and my eldest brother.

With each passing week, each passing month, each passing year I thought of my return. How? When? Who with? I have lost count of the number of times I was about to return with willing family members, close friends, old friends, new friends and a stranger or two. At the last moment I cancelled each and every arrangement. My sadness grew. I didn't realise that I had not only left my loved ones behind but also locked up all the joy Buttermere had given me for half a century.

So, why Buttermere?

My father Wladimir escaped from the Nazis in World War two. He was a Doctor. He became a refugee. He was known for his pioneering work and was given a choice. Stay in Vienna or bring all his knowledge of tuberculosis and x-ray techniques to England.

At gatherings I heard him recount the tale of the question he was asked at the British border:

"Have you come here for good?"   And my Father's reply, "I hope for better."

At twenty-two he himself contracted Tuberculosis and was given six months to live during his medical training. He went to a sanatorium in the Swiss Alps in Davos. He finally found strength in the mountain air and talked about walking on carpets of meadow flowers especially blue Gentians. In England he was posted to the industrial town of Saint Helens. One day a colleague who could feel my father's sadness said, " Doctor, I know where I must take you."

They went to Buttermere
a sanctuary to ease the mind.

View of
Buttermere's
Southern shore

Photograph by David Griffel

3

Photograph by David Griffel

Buttermere valley. My Father, Wladimir, flying a kite in the windy gap straight up to Scotland.

In April 2019 I had just cancelled yet another friend's offer of help to make the Buttermere return. I carried shame for being emotionally out of balance and for being isolated from society. I did not think I was strong enough to go back alone to a place of joy tarnished by loss. All I had were questions. I phoned a friend. She listened and her answer was simple
"Claire, the car is outside, it's a beautiful day, I'm free, let's just go."   No fuss.

Nothing to decide at last. For once, I said "Yes."

Mountains

Peaks
eruptions
from the core
heaving turmoils
to the skies.
Nests for valleys
carved by ice
to capture
tumbling mountain
water.
Coloured towers
blue
grey
gold
ginger
green
purple.
Appear clear and
go in mist.
Motionless
challenge.

Claire

The most familiar journey of my life began

I was a young child when my Father was called for from Gatesgarth farm by Sarah Annie Burns. Known as Annie, she was the owner of Wood House which nestles by the shore of Crummock Water nearer the valley entrance. Wood House was a private guest house and people arrived by word of mouth only. Recommended you could say as good guests and no trouble makers. For some years Mister Batty had stayed without leaving. Mister Batty was poorly. Everyone knew there was a foreign Doctor called Griffel who came to Buttermere with his family. Father was able to help Mister Batty. I can imagine Annie was impressed by my Father Wladimir with his unusual accent. Father I can imagine was also charmed. Not long after we were invited to stay.

Many years later I was with Annie who became my Grandmother. I was also with Jonah Todhunter, estate manager, who became my Grandfather. Annie was dying. When she died in her own little sitting room, Jonah and I were standing together, shoulder to shoulder. Within minutes of her last breath I went into the guest's sitting room and played the piano for her. I was usually shy but not at that moment. I did it without thinking. I wrote some words for her later.

Sarah Annie Burns

next to the Aga

Photograph by Mike Dobson

6

A Tune for Annie

"You are wonderful"
I told you just before you died

and when you had gone
I went into the room
to the piano you said was
difficult to play upon

I played a tune
called "Childhood Memories"

It reflected the years
as I held back all my tears
for the time that had gone

and there's hope in that tune
for you brought me back
from all my fears.

Claire

Sarah Annie Burns. A woman who had cherished and shared Wood House. She cherished me too, more than I realised. I never fully understood what it could possibly have meant for Annie, one of four sisters all childless, to offer me … me … the chance to takeover Wood House from her when I was only eighteen. I had refused. I had my sights set on adventures beyond Buttermere's mountains. I watched her in her final days wandering anxiously from room to room, distressed and asking over and over and over

"What will happen?"

Wood House
sitting room view

Photograph by
David Griffel

"All this, all this, all this?"

The last hour

We are peeling the apples.
The windfalls. To freeze.
We're keeping busy.
In the other room
She is struggling.
I've never waited before.
It comes as a surprise.
Now we stand at the side of her bed.
I am with the three friends
I've known for most of my life
And I watch while one of us dies.
Frightened to go.
The sunken face. The feverish eyes.
The grasping breath.
Teeth in the glass.
Struggles
For air.
Choking.
Knowing no-one.
"She's gone."
"No. Not yet."
"Yes that's it"
Mouth open one last time.
"Shall we shut it?"
"Can you get her teeth back in?"
"Hurry .... It will be a devil of a job otherwise."

Claire

I wrote a plea of remembrance

on 29 October 1991 which went in the Friends of the Lake District newsletter, "Conserving Lakeland."

Wood House – Memories and future thoughts

Annie Burns died on 4 October 1991 in her home,
Wood House,
on the shores of Crummock Water.
First there were the family holidays
to Annie's private guest house.
It was "private" because no advertising
was necessary.
By word of mouth, over the years,
people returned to that haven in the valley.

And now?
I hope that everyone takes great care
and thought over the sale of Wood House.
Yes, repair the roof, or the window frames.
But, please, respect and continue the years of love.
Wood House could remain as a sanctuary
from life's tearing haste."

Wood House
now and then

A glimpse of Mellbreak and Crummock Water   Knots of the past

322 BUTTERMERE

Gatekeeper on the shore road

"Ginger Poole" who opened the gate for a tip from motorists.
There was a gate keeper at Rannerdale too.

The nearer we got the clearer I could see, like covers being turned back. I chose Whinlatter pass out of the four ways into the valley.

Only when you turn round the final corner of Hause Point at the foot of Rannerdale Knots do you finally, finally see the valley length and the striking mountains of Buttermere head. Only then do you see Wood House nestling there by Crummock Water's far end shore. This was the moment I would wait for at the end of a journey. Today was no different. I had spent years thinking that all was lost. Yet I still felt the same thrill as we turned the final corner and that familiar gasp of breath and without thinking I called out

"Stop, stop, pull over please pull over. I have to get out."

HOUSE POINT, CRUMMOCK WATER

BB 302

Hause Point

Possibly this photo may include Mister Burns, Annie's Father

Beyond
Hause
point

So many things happened on the walk round Buttermere Lake that I chose to make that day.
I just sat on a tree stump opposite the valley head gazing and gazing at the mountains. So familiar.
A couple of photographers were there.
"Do you know which is the lone tree?" one asked me. It's a routine view up the valley.
"I suppose it's that one" I replied pointing to a lone tree. And before I knew what had happened
I was blurting out to the anonymous photographers that my Father's ashes,
my Mother's ashes and my eldest brother's ashes were all in the lake and I hadn't
been back for a decade. The photographers hastily moved on wishing me a good day.
I mean what would you say to that kind of announcement?

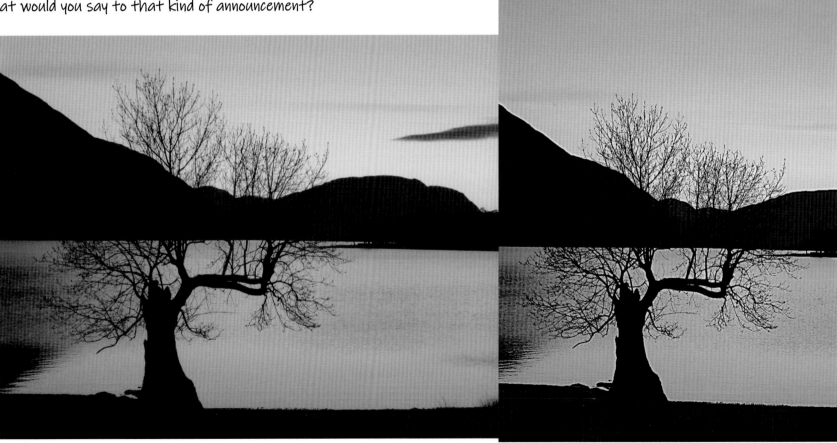

The
"other"
lone tree
under
Fleetwith

Once we had gone over the beautiful Scale bridge and walked by the lake, I looked for a place that was near the centre of the lake's length.

This special place I was searching for is in line with where Mother and I had put Father's ashes in 1984. I rowed out a boat hired from a line of wooden boats nestling on the shore near the old Ash tree. Mother carried the casket. I had felt like a captain.

"I think this is the middle" I said and stopped rowing. Mother reluctantly opened the casket and let the ashes fall into the lake. It was over in perhaps ten seconds. She cried out

"But there's so little of it so little left!"

As I stared into the lake, I saw in astonishment that my Father's ashes had spread under the water into a huge cloud with a blue tinge of colour. "Look, look how big it is. Look at how its spread. It's enormous," I called back.

For the first time in months we felt comfort and love together. At that very moment, a sharp short cutting wind flurried up from the valley head, raced across the water surface rippling the water and scuffed our cheeks. We simply stared and felt its passage.

A year later Mother and I returned on the same day in May. We stood in the place where we had launched the boat. I scattered Rosemary for remembrance and read a poem about someone being dead but still present in spirit. We cried. As our tears rolled, a strong cutting wind raced momentarily. The cold forced its way over the mountains at the valley head and across the lake … again.

Valley
head

Now here I was on my eventual return. I found the place for the remembrance ceremony that I had planned and cancelled for years. All for Father, Mother, my brother Peter, Annie and Jonah. At that moment ... strangely ... all the walkers disappeared. I felt a huge lifting relief once I finished sending my thoughts and remembrances where I wanted them to go. Abruptly a dog and his man appeared.

The dog carried an

impressive stick.

I remember his name.

Sandy

jumped into the water.

He looked up.

Triumphant!

The stick in his mouth

and

a smile on his face.

Was this what people call a rite of passage

or was I simply a passenger of time?

Views to the North   and South we arrived at Gatesgarth fields. Here my family had once camped in our canvas tent and we woke to the sound of rasping cow tongues as they happily licked off the early morning dew from the canvas.

Me and "that" horse at Gatesgarth. One of the last working horses in the valley. I fed it and it bit me. I loved it anyway.

Father and our tent

Here are the fields where I turned the hay solo in the sun with a wooden rake for Jonah Todhunter. This is the field where we ended up mending a three sided high shed and put in a new upright post. A huge "spare" telegraph pole though I am not sure where from! He wasn't to lift weights after being very ill. There was a consolation in nearly losing him that time. I received the one and only letter he ever wrote to me. It was so precious it could have been one of hundreds of letters.

Carwen Ward
Workington
Feb 4th

Dear Claire
          Grand to receive letter, also get well card a (real one) if I had got it earlier I would have been trotting around the ward by now.
I am getting along fine but not allowed out of bed as yet.
Annie & Betty come visiting pretty often even the bold Freddie.
Shall be looking forward to seeing you in the summer. the old Tractor will be getting restive,
          Best wishes
          From Old Fruit
                    Jonah.

I was Old Bean. Jonah became Old Fruit named after the first bar of chocolate he bought me. I still have the wrapper. I have no idea how I managed that!

22

Here is Char cottage belonging to Gatesgarth on the shores of Buttermere where I stayed with my parents and brother David. Father decided to build a raft. Thomas Richardson laughed his special laugh when we used some of his rope and spare leftover oil drums. And this is where I drifted solo on the raft across a sudden drop, that deep shelf under the water. I couldn't touch the bottom with my bare feet and screamed for my brother David to save me.

Char cottage

This is where we held the Buttermere show and there is the path over to Loweswater. We went to the shows there too, and sometimes to Cockermouth

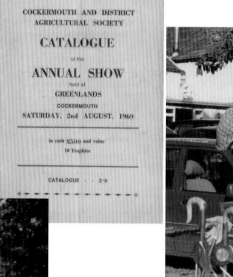

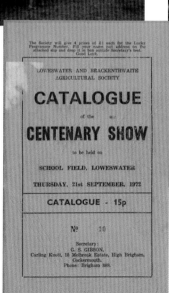

There is Red Pike and there is Sour Milk Ghyll. David and I once climbed up the Ghyll on a fine hot blue sky day and jumped into Bleaberry Tarn nestling under Red pike. The water literally took our breath away after jumping recklessly in, which must have been in our knickers. We can't remember. We emerged like rapidly leaping dolphins up through the surface gasping hysterically for breath. That was cold. I remember so well coming down High Crag screes too that day. So steep, so slippery you couldn't walk at all. Somehow we found a bounding jumping bouncing motion with each movement scattering jets of stones. I felt close to tumbling uncontrollably. Exciting and frightening in equal measures.

In 1970 I was staying at Wood House with my brother David and his Mother Eva.

David and I went up a steep ascent to go onto Red Pike and walk on the ridge towards Buttermere valley head.

I wrote letters home to my Mother and our Father when I was in Buttermere.

This short extract says it all....

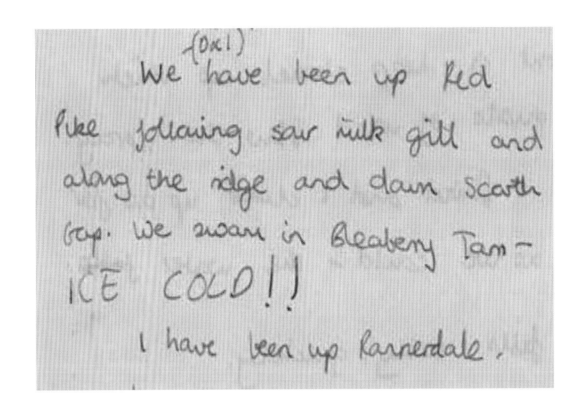

(0x1)
We have been up Red Pike following sour milk gill and along the ridge and down Scarth Gap. We swam in Bleaberry Tarn — ICE COLD!!)
I have been up Rannerdale.

Today, this day of my return, everything had significance and it all seemed just right. I thought about my eldest brother Peter Martin Griffel. I never met Peter. He died at seventeen and my brother David found Peter's ashes by my Father's bedside after Father had died. I was in a very superior mental institution, Saint Andrews hospital, where I rubbed shoulders with celebrities and aspiring stars. It was a change from some of the cuckoo's nests I had flown into and languished before leaving. My brother Peter's ashes were finally placed in Buttermere lake. I was in Saint Andrews when my psychiatrist told me my Father had died. Funny ... Saint Andrews was the name of my primary school in Preston. The first incarcerations led me into a prolonged deep depression. It was so deep that even when Father sent me to Wood House and

even when Annie did everything

to aid my return, I remained a lost spirit.

I gazed from the window in vain.

Peter

The view I could not see

26

Three's a comfort

Walking back from the ceremony I saw three birds together on Buttermere lake and imagined they represented my Father Wladimir and my Mother Dorothy and my brother Peter.

All three seemed to me to be saying we are not gone.

We are here.

Walking past
Buttermere
catkins

28

No
rowing
boats
here
now

I saw the place where a decade ago my brother David and I had put Mother's ashes. It was May 2009. We put them in Warnscale beck flowing into the lake under formidable Fleetwith Pike. Fleetwith Pike bursting with pride at being photographed and basking in relentless admiration. Fleetwith Pike looking as solid as can be and sometimes even threatening in its darkness.

I remembered Jonah telling me, to my great surprise

"Yes it's like a honeycomb inside with all the mining tunnels."

I can't look at Fleetwith without thinking of honey.

I can't look at Fleetwith without hearing my Mother telling me about the white cross up Fleetwith's flanks overlooking Gatesgarth. I had a new pair of sandals. I was about four and I was insisting that I climbed up Fleetwith with my sandals on. Why would I take off a new pair of shoes?

My Mother said

"That is a cross for a girl who she died because she wouldn't take off her new sandals when she was going up the mountain."

I can't actually remember taking off the sandals but I would imagine I did after that tale.

Fleethwith Pike in a more gentle mood

30

I couldn't return without my partner

Idrissa Sané

so I brought him the only way I could.

Buttermere Church from
Syke Farm

J.6 BUTTERMERE. "THE RETURN."

32

Now at home in Kendal after that first return, I planned the next return - a solo return on the buses. For the day.

It was about four in the morning on the day of my planned solo return. My excitement was high. I had even spent a lot of time daring to view the Wood House website. I was wide eyed to see the same dining table and chairs on one of the photos. So little yet for me so much had changed in the twenty eight years since I had stayed there. To my amazement not only was there was a room available but I booked it!

1. WOOD HOUSE, BUTTERMERE   Photo by W. E. Ball, A.R.P.S.

This postcard photo was taken when Wood House still had its huge Plane trees

The last night I had spent at Wood House I broke something!
I was sleeping in Number 7 up the back staircase, a room no longer for guests.

It was early in the morning, my last morning there and I vowed never to return after that day. I shut the window over the yard and I did it a little too hard and a pane broke. I went down very anxiously to tell Jonah and he replied

" We'll stick a bit of plastic over it ...Trust's not going to say owt [anything] "   Our last act of defiance.

Annie had left Wood House to the National Trust.

A few hours later after booking a room, here I was solo on the number 77A bus and it seemed that I was flying back.

"Can I get out at Wood House?" I asked my driver

"Stop anywhere pet."

The bus pulled away and I walked to the top gate. Same gate. Same colour. Same sign on the gate. Same latch. I put my back pack by the gate to take the photo for the memory box.

I started to pick up my back pack and as I bent down I heard it. Wrenched back through the decades. The cuckoo. The cuckoo. I could not remember the last time I heard that call. The call of echoes. What I did remember was Jonah and I standing close together in the Wood House garden listening to the cuckoo's call. Now just like then a second male cuckoo called from a different wood. The call that always made you scour the trees in the vain hope, in the strain to catch a glimpse of the bird.

Cuckoo calls

The bird dressed
in sparrowhawk clothes
to send proud parents flying.
The bird which likes to pose
as shy reclusive and yet
a secret villain daring
to wait with a gleam
to steal a hard built nest
to lay one ominous afternoon egg
to spend the rest
of spring and early summer
proclaiming its achievements
from dense leaf cover
And pairs of exhausted small birds
stretched to capacity
feed a solitary offspring
amazed by the size
of their infant
smashed egg shells and hatchlings
lie decomposing
underneath their nest
and Cuckoo calls.

Claire

Our cuckoos' hideout

As I heard the call of early days I felt old emotions swell inside me. I suddenly realised that this bird I was hearing today was a great, great, actually no idea how many greats, grandchild of our birds Jonah's and mine.

What a return. I also thought about Africa, the origin of this cuckoo and my own recent flights to and from Senegal to see my partner Idrissa and family. Yet another tale to tell.

I put my hand on the white, always white metal gate latch. The gate opened in just the way it always had. My hand opened it in just the way it always had. Walking down the top drive past the same hedge, same trees all more mature the gravel and stones making the same sound it always had. The enormous full height wooden doors to the barn where Annie kept her immaculate sky blue Morris Oxford car brought out possibly several times a year. Where Jonah kept his van, the last one white, full of bits of twine and hay and straw sheep wool, dog's hair, a wooden barrier for the occasional ewe or a gimme twinter [a young ewe in her second winter and not yet given birth] and room for me when he let me come too. Outside the barn was the long upturned rowing boat with double ratchets once cream now brown that I had rowed to the promontory on the opposite shore of Crummock. And I used to land like a pioneer on Wood House island. Only one side suitable for landing to avoid the jagged rocks on the West side.

I walked down past the same yard now with no yard gate to keep in the dogs who would by now have stopped their ferocious barking. Even when I had been away a year, the minute they smelled me the barking stopped and all those tails wagged frantically. Jonah had a way with the dogs. Local farmers in Buttermere valley and even over into Newlands and further still would phone him to ask if he could take on a dog that would not follow their shepherd's commands or ran off. Only long haired border collie Nell refused to be helped and was quite capable of following nothing else but her tail for ages and we said she was daft as a brush.

Just as I cannot see a sheep with a limp without hearing Jonah saying

"No need for that. Lazy farmer. All you need to do is put the sheep in a harness and suspend her from a beam take the wait off her feet. Soon stop limping." I know the difference between a sheep in good "fettle", or health, and a sheep in poor fettle. I can't look at a field of sheep or anything in the world around me without being guided by the voices of my ancestors and I count Jonah as one of those.

And I can hardly see a lamb without thinking of our Benjy. Benjamin. We had been checking the new born lambs. Lambing comes late to the valley. Most lambs waiting to appear in May when the weather finally begins to soften and warm. There, not far from Wood House yard, was a tiny lamb almost motionless and abandoned.

"Aye ... it's had it ... " Jonah decided and was going to walk on . I was absolutely determined that we would not join the list of those who had abandoned this creature.

"Oh please, please, please let's bring it in Oh please" on and on as only a child can do when it wants something. It is the special insistent cry of the baby which becomes the repetitive voice grinding down its decision makers.

The lamb was brought in.

Happy, I went to bed and slept really well. I had saved a lamb. Well I hoped so and in the morning rushed downstairs to the back kitchen. The lamb had made it through the night. I was also greeted by Jonah in a slightly harsh mood. After all it turned out that it was him not me who had saved the lamb with the fire burning late into the night, medicines including antibiotics to ward off the pneumonia threatening to take the lamb away. While I slept tight in my feather bed. This lamb not only recovered but grew and grew and would not stop growing. When I returned later in the year the lamb now called Benjy had developed an impressive solid body more like a Sussex sheep than the Swaledale he was. He bleated louder than any lamb I had ever heard then or since. If any of us came near his gate he called insistently. He cried for everything he had lost and everything he had been given and would often hurl himself at the gate in an effort to get more. We all loved him.

And as I walked to the main door for my first return to Wood House I saw there was no wood shed with Jonah's circular saw. And no lean-to greenhouse across the back kitchen window. I went past the same large stones and same windows along the side of the house. Past the dining room waiting for the visitors. I reached the front door. The same front door with the same top window. The same beautiful Prussian blue and crimson lake stained glass and cut glass half window. There was the same brass door handle.

Later would I find that I needed the same knack to open that door with that difficult handle? Had I forgotten the knack? Today I was a visitor. Today I rang the doorbell. I rang the doorbell for the very first time in my life. I waited. The door opened.

A man, Tony McKenzie, opened the door. Someone with a calm, friendly face, gentle enough to help me over the threshold. I held out my hand. We shook hands. The same boot stand and framed map in the hall. So much the same. The tranquillity and grace was very much intact. Even though I had seen the original dining table and chairs on the website it was still a relief to see that it was not false news. I have almost no idea what I said. I know well I can be certain that I blurted out a lot in an excitable way. Excited. Incredulous.

I was one of those visitors who claim to have been there before. The one who visited longest and most. I never forget those eager visitors who courted Annie Burns over all the years that Wood House lay in her hands. I as the youngest most regular and most popular visitor and I strutted my stuff with the air of one completely unimpressed by the guests who competed in the visitor's book.

"27th visit. Glorious as always. Many thanks "

"42nd visit" A delight to be back once more in the fold"

Or the claims at the dining table

"Yes. As Annie said to me only last night..."

"Jonah took his time to explain so much to us ... in the yard"

"Annie is definitely doing too much, as I said to her ... in the kitchen"

Competition was high to gain access into rooms and places beyond the unspoken limits of the guests' terrain. I made it surprisingly quickly and easily by endearing myself to the infamous Mister Batty who was helped during illness by my own Father's hands. From here I was invited to dry a few dishes with him in the kitchen. I was elevated to a back room girl. Things unfolded in a beautifully, quietly simple way as did almost, yes almost, every moment in that sanctuary.

This inherited "more than a visitor status" that I once used ... to walk around the house, the land and the valley, was in my mind. Today I was a guest. And so it was that I only glanced into the dining room, up the stairs, down the corridor with the door to the achingly familiar kitchen invitingly open. My glances were fleeting and perhaps not noticed.

Tony invited me into the sitting room to leave my bag to go away and check in later. It was still early morning. I walked into the room. Walking into the first room in Wood House for years. I looked through the French windows before turning to put down my bag.

Abruptly I saw the piano

that I once

played.

Before I knew what was happening

the tears came.

Tony quietly moved to the side.

Bonfire Night

Mellbreak stares into the window.
I could do the same
If I stood on Mellbreak.
I stand instead with friends
On Kendal castle's hill
and watch The Round Table firework display
I phoned him today.
He's been back to look for a certain piece of wood
he might have left behind.
Did he stand looking at Mellbreak?
Did he wonder about his hens?
Did he stop and see the spot
where foxy Reynard had paused
to look directly into the eyes
of the man who kept the hens.
Jonah Todhunter.
And I can't help it, I "ooh" and "aah"
with every throaty rocket release
with every bang echoing from the hills
And when the last blast fades
I'm here and he's there in his new home.
And Wood House stands alone.

Claire

That day I saw that Wood House was no longer alone.
The finger tight grip of long held fear filled thoughts loosened.

40

Inside Wood House

I strode out to the village. My friends the two cuckoos were still calling me. I felt beckoned.

The gate where I always waited was still the same. Same latch, same bent, curved top metal bar where I perched gazing at the glimpse of Crummock Water in the early morning waiting for the sound of boots and hooves on the metal road. While Rooks called

Thee and me

Overnight the crevasses on the fells have been painted
Leaving white dribbles on the slopes.
At the valley head the sun struggles over somber hill tops.
A low ribbon of mist threads across high Fleetwith
And catches pink light in reflection
As the sun finally casts its bloomed shafts over the crag.
The mountain bracken throws its gingered tone
Into the quivering depths of the lake.
She crouches on the gate top to wait.
A sudden movement horrifies two sheep.
Up jerk their heads to contemplate the intruder.
They stare - with munching mouths and glass eyes.
Soon returning, forgetful, to the sweet meadow grass.
A man's hobnail boots strike the road's surface
And the fellsides fling back the clacking sound...
She hears the piercing yelp of a dog.
Several contented cows peer hesitantly round the road's corner
Hastily pushed forward by the dog as it skims from side to side.
She opens the gate - the cows pass through
Eyelashes fluttering and udders swaying, they trot away.

Man, dog and girl walk on together.
Wagtails bob over the meadow
And in larch trees chaffinches slip from branch to branch
As if they were Autumn's cast-off leaves.

Claire 1970

I walked straight across and down that very same field. I walked through the bluebell wood to the car park built on a water meadow belonging once to Esther Burns at Cragg Farm. I lingered in the woods rapt in the beauty of new green leaves, blue flowers and sunshine. I peered over the wall into the garden. I imagined I heard voices echoing, Esther, Winnie and Grace, Annie's sisters, and their parents. I noticed I had started to walk with a jaunt. I did it even more when tourists, visitors went past. Exactly as I did years ago. I live here. I'm a local and this is my place and you are just being allowed here for a moment in time.

4295. POST OFFICE, BUTTERMERE.
Lowe, Patterdale Copyright

Cragg Farm as Buttermere post office run by the Burns family

Cragg Farm today

44

So in that style I almost swaggered into the Fish Inn.

Jonah had once told me a tale about leaving a trail of fish roe from the beck to the buildings.

FISH HOTEL AND SOUR MILK GHYLL.
ABRAHAMS SERIES.

46

Transcript of Jonah Todhunter talking after seeing the postcards of the Fish Hotel recorded by me in 1990

Jonah: Aye there was yance [once] we got a lot of salmon out of ... salmon used to come to this beck. An' me and Tom Edmonson ... I used to hold lamp for him. We'd, we'd a ... to catch salmon when its dark you know ... and he had a bicycle lamp carbine. You've heard tell of bicycle lamp made of carbine. Well it was that. And you shone it on your fish. Yan [one] fella shone it on fish. Fish was stationary and t'other fella click out. I used to hold lamp and Tom used click 'em out. Got two that night. And ... Tom he was t'other side of beck and I was yan side beck, him t'other and he fished up this yan about ten pounds. He hooked it and he got, he got it ... pulled up off bloody rocks and he lost his feet ont' rocks and he fell in the bloody beck did Tom and the bloody fish got off. I always remember that. He hit a bloody clatter like.

Claire: What sort of fish?

Jonah: Salmon. Well they come to spawn. If you get them out of the beck before they spawn they're good but once they spawned they're no good. They've gone soapy. They're not meat. Once they've gone up to spawn and you catch them going back you can forget about it. When you catch them coming up to spawn they're good fish. Aye, I got one fish out here just under.. just screw o' the bridge. I got out and I come out on that .. come out onto shore an', and I went down Fish front with it into the, into that what did they call it ... it's a stable and following morning I could see where I'd been ... there was salmon spawn up the ... all the way up the bloody Fish front. Just like split peas. See, I should of held it by the bloody tail. Now I just had my hand in its gill and I carried it and tail was hanging down and of course up from tail its where they get shot [rid] of the eggs. Halfway between the belly and the tail is the hole you see and spawn all come out. I swept it up afterwards. From ... bloody ... the beck you could have followed where that fish was in the stable like you see what I mean. Oh aye could have been caught out like.

Claire: You left a trail all the way home.   *Jonah: Exactly.*

I could hardly wait to eat and get back to Wood House and go into Room 1 for the first time in my life.

I had slept in all the rooms up the back staircase except Annie's minute space under the eaves.

Number 4 was my absolute favourite with its view of the woods and up the steep sided fells all the way to Red Pike. Such a mysterious fell. From a certain angle looking South from Buttermere lake's shore Red Pike looks low and gentle and looking North from the Loweswater end of Crummock Water the peak looks challenging and domineering.

All the rooms had basins and the beds had satin covered light green or pale blue eiderdowns and crisp white cotton sheets that had hung outside on the washing line near the vegetable garden and fruit trees. They dried on the maiden up near the ceiling by the fire in the back kitchen. When I was there we shook the sheets straight ... Betty and I, inside by the fire .

Best of all I was able to choose what time I wanted to wake up when I stayed there.

I was really proud of this skill. I would bang my head firmly on my pillow. So if I wanted to wake up at the precise time I had chosen say 7, I would bang my head 7 times. I got so good at this that I could even do half hours. This involved a more gentle bash on the pillow.

Sweet dreams, sweet days.

Now here I was.

I had graduated to the front staircase. I was a pensioner with rights and a history.

I almost flung open the door and I claimed my room clutching the sandwiches for later so I could stay in Room 1 from late afternoon until breakfast time.

Graduate in room 1

This time I could see the view ... even my African Swallow had arrived

49

The setting sun beyond the valley gap gave way to the moon

I woke before dawn.

And so began an extraordinary morning vigil. There on the red velveteen chair and nothing between me and the view.

I took part as in a vivid dream in the lap of absolute luxury. That's what I had. I wasn't wild camping. AND I had a huge furry blanket, thoughtfully provided. I was wrapped up in the morning chill. I took photo after photo with gaps in between to gasp, to laugh, to cry out. [Quietly! After all, others were sleeping]

There was just the hint of morning and I watched a magical spectacle unfold. I was sure I had never seen Crummock so beautiful, golden gleaming becoming more and more intense. The sun swooped down over Mellbreak and brought colour to another day.

50

That
morning
the
pattern
of trails
in the
sky
surprised
me.

51

Sunlight creeping down Mellbreak's flanks and shimmering on Crummock Water

53

And there is the triangle reflected. "Never goes away" said Jonah

I arrived for breakfast and sat once more at that so familiar table.

I couldn't help but remember Mister Batty always at the head of the table. Rotund, he kept a very firm control of proceedings. The guests knew that at the very moment the last person had put down their spoon or fork or knife Mister Batty would gesture. With both arms raised above his head slightly bent at the elbow fingers curled slightly with the hint of a smile on his face, he gestured with a rather insistent beckoning movement. We all obediently and promptly passed up our empty dishes to form a neat pile.

Betty arrived when summoned by the bell.

When I was at the table I was allowed without question to ring the bell. I would look intently at Mister Batty who now sat behind the pile of plates. He would nod almost imperceptibly. Nod is not really the word for it. He bowed slightly, very slightly and up I jumped to ring the bell.

Within seconds Elizabeth Coulthard, Betty, arrived and we all craned our heads to see what delights were laden on the trolley's top shelf.

On the trolley at breakfast time there was homemade porridge and the leftovers were feasted upon by the hens in Hen House Wood.

Also on the trolley at breakfast time there was a traditional English cooked breakfast including those Hen House Wood eggs. All sorts of products were brought in local delivery vans and carried in baskets into the back kitchen from Cockermouth shops and cooked using the enormous Aga.

And there on the table by the front stairs the guests could find their packed lunches. There were all sorts of sandwiches made with Esther Burns home cooked bread and cut finer than anyone could cut. I would stand and gaze as Betty expertly cut slice after slice of excruciatingly thin bread so you had more filling in your sandwiches than dough. With a choice of fruit and a slice of Annie's fruit cake just in case.

This was where guests would find their flasks filled with coffee and little packets of sugar cubes wrapped in greaseproof paper. Everything was wrapped in paper. Coming home [I mean back to Wood House] down off the fells by 4 pm would give you enough time to freshen up. Then the trolley would return groaning with home cooked afternoon tea. All this to sustain the weary walkers before dinner.

Betty, Jonah Annie, with the dogs being camera shy

From the cold tap came the purest water on Earth.

It came from a natural spring up in the Larch wood leading up onto the flanks of Rannerdale Knots opposite the lower white gate. The one that opened and closed for me throughout my early years. Sometimes we used to go, Jonah and I, to clean out the filter. It was so beautiful that even before I tasted wine I knew that water tasted better than wine. One of my parting treasures to take home was my flask filled with it. It was the best water I have ever drunk in my entire life. It became my prize because in amongst my tears on each and every final day of any visit I would fill my flask with the precious liquid.

The car, the bus, the trains and another car had dragged me away back to my childhood home and homes of later life.

I would have a little of that water and would feel a bit better.

In the early mornings Annie would already be sitting with a first cup of tea and a biscuit ready to start the day's work. Only Annie was small enough to fit into her under the eaves room and as her back bent over with long days, she fitted into her room even more easily with the knack of ages as she shrunk.

I am the proud owner of her bedside table.

I have the two Sunday trifle dishes. One was once for the Wood House guests and the smaller one was used to take up to Cragg Farm for Esther and Joe Benn.

By my own bed is Annie's small wooden box with a sliding cover over two compartments and inside is Annie's tiny gold watch to fit her tiny wrist.

On top of the box I have her little mother of pearl silver bladed penknife.

Annie gave me the books that she, Annie, Esther and Winnie 3 of the 4 Burns sisters won as school prizes.

Buttermere School

60

Close up view of the pupils

Best of all I have the most beautiful painting by Annie, painted when was she was sixteen. It is of Scale Force waterfall above Crummock Water and was done on brown paper.

It was floating onto the floor to be added to a pile.

Betty and Jonah and I sat at the table to go

through Annie's papers after she had died.

The air was heavy.

The painting floated onto the floor

towards the pile to throw away.

I snatched it up to treasure.

I had it framed.

The painting has been

on the walls

of my homes ever since.

I knew after my first night back in Wood House that another part of my Buttermere return was a visit to Scale Force once more.

I have some of Annie's handwritten music notations. She played the organ for over 50 years and bought the organ. Find it in the Church of Saint James as you go out of Buttermere village up Newlands to Keswick. There is a little commemorative plaque on its side. Before that Annie played the old organ and pushed the pump pedals in and out with sheer determination .

Annie's transcriptions for Magnificat

sung at evensong in Saint James

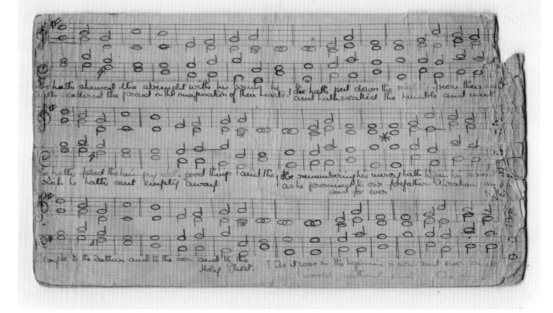

Jonah was Church warden. He tolled the bell to call us.

Church Warden

My good friend Jonah Todhunter was so proud indeed
When presented with the key to the Parish Church vestry door
Going each Sunday an hour before
With the cold red wine tasting of vinegar
On communing tongues.
In his Sunday best it is he
Who calls the congregation together
With a bell which has rung
More than a hundred years
And now the candles alight he sits at the back
With Freddie in the not so hushed exchange
Of the racing results and local news
Amateur registrars of losses and gains.
To me he confided his disappointment at the inaugural ceremony
All the way to Workington to be initiated.
The hens fed, fires cleaned and laid
Aga and stove prepared, cats and dogs, wood chopped
And an early wash, with good clothes and trouble parking.
All the way to Workington and the same trouble again
With each annual renewal for a two minute ceremony
And no bite to eat not even a sup
And it's a shame he's decided he will not stand again.

Claire   [1988/1993 revised]

64

Buttermere Church and Crummock Water.

Abraham's Series No. 934, Keswick.

65

Mister White at Buttermere was a very different sort of vicar. Mister White liked chocolates, liked a whisky and I know he discussed racing results with Jonah. Best of all he didn't climb up even the few steps of Saint James' pulpit. He sat with his legs crossed on an ordinary kitchen chair in front of the altar and not only that I actually knew what he was talking about in the sermon. Betty and I sat together in Church and behind us sat Jonah and Freddie. Annie sat at the organ her feet just touching the huge pump pedals. We decorated the Church at flower festival time from her beloved garden.

I remember once sitting with a bunch of dried honesty grown by Annie. She set Betty and I to work on the back kitchen table, polished every morning. We had to peel off the two outer layers very carefully so as not to tear the precious inner. That inner shines like silk. We were rewarded with a coffee made from Camp coffee essence and unpasteurised milk given to us by the Cragg farm cows ... we call it raw milk today! Their pasture by Wood House back garden was the reward for parting with their milk.

To get to the Cows' gate in time I used my pillow banging technique for waking, checked the weather, chose the right clothes, raced downstairs, flew up to the top gate, then I was ready to stroll along the road by the white metal railings. I heard the fell-magnified calls of the rooks, fell-magnified calls of sheep and in the right season, from May in the valley, lambs crying. My mood changed and sometimes I could marvel at the delights of sunrise or shudder under the wind and clouds or huddle against the rain just to sit with relentless determination on the top of the cows' gate. Those cows were pretty choosy about who could milk them and whose hands could be placed directly on their udders. I wasn't allowed to go into the small milking parlour at Cragg Farm - not even to stand at the byre door lingering as I wished to do. All just in case the cows obstinately refused to give up their milk in front of a stranger who definitely didn't smell right. The milk was separated by Jonah standing with calm routine turning the handle of the separator as I watched the cream pouring from one spout and the remaining milk from the other. I loved to carry the milk home with Esther's fresh bread and butter wrapped in cotton cloth.

The next essential event after waiting on the gate was going to Hen House wood. We all went. Jonah led the way with a bucket full of delights for the hens. The hens were enchanted by Jonah's secret recipe for their breakfast which of course included that leftover porridge.

My vow never to return to Wood House was broken. That vow itself felt as if it was a distant echo of past loss. All these memories and many more precious memories came flowing back to me.

Times past

Turning the
hay at
Rannerdale

Jonah
hedging
near
Wood
House
low
gate

Father the farm hand

Jonah ready for work

Wood House yard
with the back doors
of the huge two
storey barn open

Joe Benn from Cragg Farm in the cows' field near Wood House vegetable garden

Everyone's
return
from
the
hens with
Jonah

During that 24 hours of my first solo return I had spoken only to one person in the outside world and that was Idrissa in Senegal.

At Wood House as in most of Buttermere valley there was no mobile network. It was amazing for me not to be connected and to have no phone line. Could I really sense emptier airwaves? I liked the taste of being unreachable for good reason. The power of being. The quietness was almost overwhelming.

But more overwhelming to me was the connection I felt with my old self. The one who had spent all that time in the valley. The one who was me before I was so ill so many times and so often during forty years of adult life. The one of unsound mind.

During that first return I found no hint of a troubled, distressed, disturbed mind. Instead I found the hope of my youth and I found that hope had not left me at all but was there all along in disguise and hidden as if camouflaged.

The whole of my first solo return had a domino like effect.

I awakened from years of medicated slumber to agree with myself that the days of proving my sanity were over. I meant each and every day of doing this to anyone I encountered whether they were familiar, family, or strangers were no longer required. Even if this was going to take some practice, those days were at an end.

I was officially a pensioner.

I would be an outspoken one. Personal freedom to act as me.

To be me.

I took the bus back over Honister pass back to Keswick and another bus back to Kendal.

Back over Honister Pass with dramatic bursts and rays of sunshine through the clouds

74

Less than 2 weeks later after that solo return, I had arranged to visit the valley again to see Betty with a friend for the day.

Betty and I had been very close. The only time I saw her cry was once when I had been allowed to stay an extra week making three in all. Betty cried when I was leaving. I was staying for two weeks and as the time began to run out an air of melancholy settled over us all - Annie, Betty Jonah and I in the back kitchen. Not even playing dominoes on the round table, polished every day by Annie, could cure us.

We played for money at a penny a game. I brought the dominoes which went up to double nine and I also brought the money. The same 1p coins each time, wrapped up in paper bag from the chemists. And we would very seriously get more and more excited with each penny won.

Jonah would sigh   "I'm dicky up the bloody orchard now"

Or "Got rid of my currant cake"

"Heavy metal" with another sigh

"I can go ... just "

After we had been knocking on the table and couldn't go

"This'll let you out"   or   "Pump you buggars ... pump"

and   "What shall I do to be saved?"

Even though we had heard his exclamations so many times before, as each of them came out during the pauses they would catch us off guard. Betty and I would get a worse and worse case of the giggles until we were all laughing including Annie and finally Jonah and just the writing of it to you now gives me the warmth of that memory.

As well as seeing Betty on my third return visit, I also wanted to see Annie's and Jonah's graves in Lorton church yard. I always know where Jonah's small stone is. He was cremated. Annie was buried with her family. Every time I have been to her grave I take ages to find it. This time was no different.

The Church clock struck obligingly as I finished tending the graves.

The same posies for both graves and all recycled by me from a Kendal Chapel's bin.

Father taught me about recycling and using what people throw away.

Funny that every time I go now to find
the Burns' family graves I get lost and
can't find my way.

I wrote home in the 1970s
about the same trouble!

4

asked him to go to the churchyard & cut
the grass around the Nelson's graves (Mrs
Burns was a Nelson - I didn't realise) &
he wasn't too pleased about it. He had no
idea where the graves were so Annie drew
him a map. Anyway we found (amidst the
overgrown mass) Annie's parents' & sisters' graves
& had great difficulty in finding the others.
We were arguing (he was swearing, as usual)
& and wandering about. In the end we
found one gravestone for Nelsons and we just
cut the nearest graves around it. It was
so funny — he kept getting out this map
and angrily exclaiming that the graves were
nothing like it. After all how is he
expected to find graves in the middle of a
bloody meadow ?! I managed to calm him
down and he cheered up when we found

Next I had arranged to visit Elizabeth Coulthard who we called Betty. She is one of two survivors from the Wood House I was part of when Annie was alive. The other is Mary, Betty's sister, is also alive. Mary had worked at Wood House before she married. My dear friend Betty who was given time off to go to Workington with me when I was about fourteen. There was time off to look round the shops and money for our lunches from Annie.

I hadn't seen Betty for 27 years. We always exchanged cards at Christmas and birthdays.

This time, Betty took us out to lunch at Loweswater because she said it was a special day. We shared memories. We laughed and there were tears in our eyes of sadness and gladness. Here was another connection that was not lost but regained. I will be back I said when we parted.

Later, my friend and I went to meet Tony Mckenzie at Wood House and I had the massive treat of sitting in the back kitchen.

"My" back kitchen was a memory no longer for siting and playing dominoes, folding sheets, betting on the horses, doing the accounts or watching the television with transmission quality like sitting in a snow storm. Now it was a modern cooking kitchen. I got to sit in the kitchen behind the scenes once more, never dreaming it could happen. I never even had the thought that I could agree to do it again!

And Tony, seeing how moved I was, told me that this room was also a very special room for him and all his family. This very room had seen twenty five years of their own family gatherings at Christmas.

Then, very quietly, in came a gentle woman. I found myself meeting Tony's mother who clearly showed her own love of Wood House. I had only once ever seen that depth of love before ... in Annie's eyes.

We went for a walk in Rannerdale afterwards.

The famous Rannerdale bluebells were still out. We enjoyed their beauty unexpectedly, as it was already the third week in May.

I wondered what funny phrase Jonah would have given to this ewe who struck a pose and seems to have big ideas about the right sort of bed to rest on!

The blueness was soothing. It had been another enormous day.

I found my way to Rannerdale one Autumn when I was still at school. It kept me captive then too

Autumn Valley

The beck was pouring down the valley
A white torrent
Rowan trees bowed down
Laden heavy with their fruit

The sun was riding high in the sky
Casting its rays upon the valley
Lighting up its secret entrance
Lying hidden by Rannerdale knots

The bracken had turned golden bronze
There were cinnamons, gingers, and ochres
The earthy colours were alive with the sun
Glowing against the somber fells

I chanced upon this Autumn valley
And sat in quiet contemplation
The sight cleared my aching mind
The gift of life just for you and me

Claire

Now, at the end of this visit, my friend asked,

"Which pass do you want to go over to go home?"

I always imagined I would take myself back over Newlands pass to go home if I ever, ever returned. Drive myself. It was my favourite way to arrive and to leave.

There was a special view close to my heart immediately near Bear Falls at the back of Robinson below the ever soggy Buttermere Moss. Bear Falls is reputed to be the sighting of the last wild bear in England about 500 years ago.

Park the car and walk to the edge of the land above Buttermere valley.

Here you can see a sliver of a glimpse of Crummock Water nestling in the valley. That view meant to me that I had nearly arrived at Wood House. And going home, I would stop and stand at the same spot to bid my farewell. And I can now say ... I still do.

There were and still are many ways to arrive in the valley.

These photo postcards were taken in the early days of the first tourists.

THE ASCENT FROM BORROWDALE TO HONISTER 603. MAYSONS KESWICK

The long climb up Honister pass

Honister pass, then an unmade road, descending into Buttermere Valley

2061. HONISTER CRAG AND PASS.   JUDGES'

The descent with no luxury for keen tourists

Jonah and I recorded tapes for this book. I had asked Annie first. It took courage to ask as it felt like an intrusion. She smiled with a knowing look and refused. Jonah was happy to do it. I had waited a while before asking him. I had built up a collection of old postcards of the valley. We looked at them together while Jonah talked. I remember being so impressed when I showed him my postcard of horses and carriages climbing out of the valley up Newlands pass. They climbed up just past Saint James Church opposite the all-powerful Sour Milk Ghyll.

Jonah recognised the coach driver and said:

"Aye that's Jack Porter - he drove for the Lake Hotel him int' grey top hat.

There was a Johnny Porter used to live at Rannerdale.

Jack Porter was his Uncle.

They called him Johnny Porter and they called him John Porter so they always called him Jack.

All Johns is Jacks really.

Aye. It's very good is that.

They're all having to bloody walk eh? Silly old buggars."

Going back
to Keswick

See the
grey top
hat of the
driver

533. COACHING UP BUTTERMERE HAUSE.
(ABRAHAMS' SERIES.)

111 "THE DEVIL'S ELBOW."
COACHES RETURNING FROM
BUTTERMERE TO KESWICK.
(ABRAHAM'S SERIES)

I hadn't seen Betty since Jonah's funeral at Lorton. He died on New Year's day in 2002. I had visited him in the cottage hospital in Keswick and visited him again in Workington when he didn't recover well enough. That time when I visited him I knew he was dying. He thought my then partner was his nephew and talked about a black dog - a symbol seen as a herald of endings. I held his hands and saw the distance in his eyes. I knew this was the final physical goodbye. I was the last person he talked to. I thought that was a very special gift.

In 2002 I wrote another article for Friends of the Lake District's magazine, Conserving Lakeland:

Jonah Robinson Todhunter... If you know Buttermere Valley, there's the mountain called Robinson. Named after Jonah Robinson who was known as John. He was Jonah's Great Uncle and a pioneer rock climber. He was one of the first men to climb Pillar Rock in Ennerdale and the Buttress at Scafell Pike ... And then there's Todhunter – Foxhunter

Before I knew Jonah, as a young man he was a redhead. He was one of the first men to own a motorbike in Buttermere Valley. He was a particularly good waltzer and young women wanted to partner him at dances. He would say he just knew a trick or two, especially on competition nights when he said he made a point of dancing near the judges' table. His first job was an Ostler for The Fish Hotel. He worked as a Shepherd and Farm Hand all over the Lake District ... He settled finally at Wood House on the shores of Crummock. Here he worked for the rest of his life for Miss Annie Burns ... I followed Jonah everywhere I could. All I wanted to do was to go out on "jobs" with him. I argued my case, for gathering sheep ["You'll strain your ankles"]; to pack wool ["Your hands will be terrible greasy"]; to rebuild a shed ["It's heavy work"]; to go stone walling ["There'll be nowt to do"]; to go hay making [You'll get thirsty and hot"]. I usually persuaded him to let me come too.

He taught me so much. He told me stories and tales and local history. He taught me to drive a tractor, to grow potatoes, to turn hay, to land the boat on Wood House Island. He taught me to love all the living things in the valley. He showed me my one and only Snow Goose. Above all he showed me a quiet, uncritical acceptance of life.

And for all these things, I know how truly lucky I am. Jonah worked right up to Annie's death weaving a beautiful Larch fence for Wood House driveway and going up ladders to paint even in his mid-eighties ... Jonah died on 1st January 2002. He was 97. On 7th January I waited for the very last time for Jonah; and just as he was carried into my view all I could hear were a few rooks. It is with all this in mind that I feel able to make a plea and a request. My plea is for us … to keep an ever more vigilant eye on the Buttermere Valley. **Claire Griffel**

The funeral is a blur. I didn't speak but was bursting with things to say. It was dry and sad. The memories were shining and singing and I wrote this instead

Crummock

The water lay still and calm

The sun's diamonds glittering on its surface

The air was filled with the smell of new mown hay

Seagulls called with plaintive cries

Silver fish jumped for helpless flies

Goat-eyed sheep munched fell side grass

Swarms of gnats twisted spirals by the shore

A heron beat its passage across the sky

The evening drew peacefully on

The sun sank low over the shimmering valley

The velvet water glowed with crests of peach

A Canada goose called goodnight.

Claire

And still the bells toll

Friday 6 March 1992 ... after a long silence

THE WEST CUMBERLAND
TIMES and STAR

West Cumberland Journal   Friday, March 6, 1992   PRICE 29p

Ding dong dale back in tune

THE sound of church bells will echo across the beautiful Buttermere valley this Sunday after a long silence.

The two bells at St James' Church were taken away to be renovated and tuned last year after 150 years faithful service.

On Monday they were welcomed back by vicar, Michael Braithwaite, and the two church wardens.

A host of parishioners also gathered outside the tiny fellside church to see the bells returned and to capture the moment on film.

Rev Braithwaite said the bells were taken down when work began rebuilding the tower, which had acquired a lean of

three inches over the years.

The unmatched bells — the oldest of which was made in 1766 and pre-dates the existing church by 74 years — were tuned and had their stocks and clappers replaced.

The work was carried out by the specialist firm, Taylors of Lough-bor-

ough, and the bells were transported free of charge by Lawson's Haulage from Cockermouth.

Jim and Eileen Lawson were married at St James' Church more than 30 years ago. Eileen, whose maiden name was Clarke, was brought up in Buttermere, where her parents ran the village Post Office. She was also christ-

ened at the church, as were her three children.

Mr Lawson said: "When I heard that the church faced the added expense of having to have the bell refurbished, I thought the least I could do was to offer to provide free transport for them."

Church secretary, Alan Johnson, said the whole job, including re-furbish-

ing the bells, had cost around £7,000.

He explained: "We hope people will come forward and help us pay this bill, which is certainly more than can be met by the collection from the congregation."

● Pictured are, from the left, Jim Lawson, warden Jonah Todhunter, Rev Michael Braithwaite and warden Freddie Rayson.

90

Saint James Church in 2020

Jonah with Mary, Betty's sister, when she also

worked at Wood House

Jonah with an adoring dog and

you can just see his tractor in its shed in the old barn

The Larch fence woven by Jonah in his mid-80's for Wood House lower driveway

After seeing Betty again, I saw only one way forward in my return and I booked 7 nights at Wood House. It was way beyond my budget, but was there a price on this? The bus climbed up Honister pass once more with me and a the burning desire to write again.

The 77a bus up Honister coughed and spluttered behind an endless stream of cyclists on a challenge. The bus company was determined to get the tourists into the valley. The passengers complained bitterly about the cyclists. I expect the cyclists did the same. At the top of Honister, the bus refused to stop beeping its warning with an overheated gear box. We waited for it to cool down. Some passengers even went to the shop and got lost and I ran off to find them. My heightened excitement made me think I would walk to Wood House if I had to from the top of Fleetwith Pike where we nestled. But before long we were racing faster than any cyclist down the pass. We flew past sheer grey blue slate mounds, chiselled rock faces and enormous boulders torn from their perch and stranded by weather and gravity. So huge that you could almost wince in case one unexpectedly had enough of a little shove to make it carry on its descent from the heights and crush us all in the 77a.

I made a now almost regular and even recognised request to get out at Wood House. The next and very first morning I came downstairs early before breakfast into the sitting room near the piano and began writing. I could hardly believe it.

Those seven days and nights had a quality that perhaps people find when they go on a retreat or on a course of multivitamins or perhaps both. I tasted, again, the excitement of waking with "that view".

I could get up early in those May days and be ahead of all the visitors and relish the tranquillity and bask in being there. No more virtual memories arose to taunt me from far away, from long ago.

Yes, I fumed at the arrival of litter. I made a pile in Hen House Wood. I phoned the Friends of the Lake District and the National Trust and told them where the pile was. I phoned the National trust to complain about the jetty where we used to launch the Wood House boats. I have no idea how many times how many hours I spent on the jetty. It was on my list of essential first things to do with each visit through the garden gate and down the side of the woods. It was here I stood and sometimes sat and daydreamed. It was here that I launched one of the two boats to row out across Crummock Water.

The wooden boat I
rowed

now resting by the
old barn front

It was from the landing that Jonah amazed the household by taking me fishing.

His best friend had died and they always used to go out on the lake to catch the sweetest fish - the deep water Char. His friend died and Jonah stopped fishing. Betty told me what a special honour it was for him to take me.

I was now free to go anywhere to walk anywhere and everywhere and took endless photos perhaps not just for remembrance but just in case I lost something once more.

Crummock Water

The rocks where I
played

The comfort of Crummock curves during my return

and

Mill Beck rushing to pass into Scale Beck

Comfort from a
natural heart in Mill
Beck

Comfort in winged beauty

Going solo

Gazing male Mallard

Wait for me
Canada geese in a row with a
with a fourth beak just appearing

Comfort in everything

Horizons far

and by our feet

100

Comfort in making things

Dewdrop on
Buttermere woods path

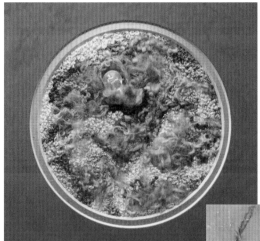

Buttermere woods

Buttermere shore

101

Comfort in natural beauty

Valley head

Crummock evening and a

Mallard duckling in a race to join the family

Part of my seven day return was a trip to Cockermouth where Jonah was born. I have no idea how many times we made that trip in whichever van he was driving over the years. I remembered a thriving important market town with a Farmer's Auction. A town full of life. We collected Jonah's winnings from his daily bets on the horses. I studied and learned form. I knew which trainers did well. I knew not to bet on races with the same brothers in ..."Fixed". I knew which horses came from far away so best to avoid that race ... "Tricky" I knew which horses not to bet on ... "O'er the hill" and ... "O'er the hill and far away". I remember when the call was placed on the phone, the landline, "Todhunter, Buttermere, twenty two shilling yankee each way." [a bit more than one pound]

I wanted to see the "Black Bull" again where Jonah was born. It was still there. It seemed to me no accident that Jonah was born in the Black Bull.

His working life was spent almost entirely in Cumberland and Westmorland. He remembered the hirings where you lined up to be chosen for work.
He remembered working for Beatrix Potter at Yew Tree farm in Coniston, "Bad tempered old biddy." He remembered working up at Watendlath, "Back of beyond."
He also told me stories of his time in the army medical corps when he did go into Scotland. I have his training manual which he gave me.
He also had a job for two brothers when he wanted a taste of another county. He went all the way to the contrasting lands of Norfolk.
I will never forget the story about a tribe of rats who made him stop as he walked from one farm to the other.

"I heard a chattering high pitched. I stopped for what felt like 5 minutes and a sea of rats crossed the road in front of me. I was stock still. Never moved. You wouldn't dare distract them like. They were moving from one haystack to the next."

The other Norfolk story was about no less than ... a Black Bull!

"Aye it was because of a black bull that I had to come home. I had always been friendly with one of the brother's bulls. A black bull. One day for no apparent reason that black bull turned on me when I was putting down his feed and mauled me. Badly. Nearly to death. It was on account of that black bull that I came back to Cumberland"

It was on account of that black bull that I knew Jonah - the pub as well as the Norfolk animal.

104

Main Street, Cockermouth

105

Wood House
Buttermere Cockermouth.

Dear Dr Griffell   Tuesday night.

Thank you for your letter and cheque – I'm sending back the cheque for you to destroy, I'm sorry I quite forgot to give it to Claire as we arranged! We did enjoy having her and hope that you will allow her to come again before too long. The hay was finished yesterday (Monday) and the menfolk say it is quite good quality, We have had 3 really marvellous days with lots of sunshine – very welcome after the wet spell. Jonah has been

I thought of my journeys to Wood House in 1960s and 70s, once my family moved to Oxfordshire. There was a car from my village to Banbury station to go on the train, full of drunk travellers. Next change at Carlisle and walk from the rail station to the bus station. Change at Wigton. Arrive at Cockermouth to be met nearly always by Jonah. I was by then at secondary school and a fully-fledged member of the back kitchen. Only sometimes would Annie put her foot down and insist that I ate with the real guests. "You are not having the leftovers. Your Father wouldn't be very pleased." I didn't care and anyway these were my holidays and I was invited by Annie to stay. I will never forget the first time when Annie refused payment from my Father for my stay. No words. I will also never forget the time when I had already stayed for two full weeks and we were all so sad that I was about to go home. Annie surprisingly phoned my father to ask for a week's extension. I was in a daze.

She spoke well as she always did, with gentle but persuasive charm. A call from Buttermere to Oxfordshire was definitely classed as long distance and surprising, unless urgent. Annie finally said, "Goodbye Doctor" and turned to us with a thumbs up.
I was staying another week.
No charge for that.
My graduation week.

During these later trips I learned so much. I helped to get the sheep off the higher fells to come down to the lower pastures for dipping and shearing. I packed wool with Jonah and Joe. Joe and I handed the fleeces to Jonah. The enormous hessian sacks were suspended from the high beams of the front barn at Cragg farm. A large stone in each corner wrapped around and secured by rope and strung up. Jonah stood on the three-legged milking stool straddling the sack, one leg in the sack one leg out. Years ago the Herdwick and Swaledale fleeces were worth good money and now even in the 1970s it was hardly worth it. Only the white fleeces made money. Nowadays, I am surprised how much fleeces are sold for in the tourist shops.

Generous parent

Lazy

afternoon

Three Tup comfort. Rams in limbo longing for the mating season

Hay making time was special.
I pretended not to notice the sometimes admiring [adults] sometimes envious[children] glances as I stood nonchalantly with my "been doing this all my life" attitude on the back of grey Fergy ... Jonah's Ferguson model tractor. We even made the number plate for a trailer. Jonah cut the wood on his circular saw in the wood shed. You passed through the wood shed on the way to the washing line and to the fruit and vegetable gardens I drew the numbers and letters on the wood and painted them. I thought it was my trailer.
I learned to drive on old Fergy.

Old Fergy

I learned to drive
on Old Grey Fergy
Jonah taught me
driving through the village
passing the tourists
a smile on my face
to show I'd been doing this
all my life
A local girl
on old grey Fergy
bringing in the hay
and using the clutch and gears
just right so the bails didn't
wobble
sipping Esther's lemonade
at each unloading
proud to be
part of the
haymaking gang.
Claire

Jonah and Fergy on Annie's birthday in my birth year!

Better still, I got so good that I was even allowed to drive the tractor in the hayfields at haymaking. Sid Clark usually did that. Sid Clark was the valleys' road sweeper. You didn't have blocked drains blocked by Autumn's cast off leaves in those days. Sid Clark smoked a pipe. He had an indent, a curve in his false teeth where his pipe could sit all day talking or not. Talking mainly. No one could talk like Sid Clark. He lived in the row of cottages opposite Cragg Farm and Mrs Clark took over the running of Buttermere post office. It was once run by the Burns at Cragg Farm. Sid Clark could talk until tomorrow. He loved my Father. They talked a lot. I heard them talk about a whisky smuggler called Moses Rigg one day ... another secret of Fleetwith Pike.

Moses Rigg's home

A detailed letter from Annie to me in 1970 with news

Wood House Buttermere

My dear Claire   Sunday. 9.53
            Just had supper after
coming in from Church — Jonah
now sitting studying the Sunday
paper — and Betty almost asleep..
They don't know I've started this
to you — we were all delighted
with your letter and the photograph
They are very good. and it is
nice to have the ones of your home
and your bedroom window — Hay
was finished shortly after — you
left — and I know the newyorks
missed your help. It really was

wonderful how the weather just
lasted at that time. until they
got it all into the barn — in
the field — we've had some lovely
weather since — and even now it is
quite good but cooler. Trish likes
it better he isn't panting so much.
Jess is very much more at home
and barks at every noise — she
allows me to pet her now. We've
had several folks staying with
dogs — two at once — but fortunately
they didn't quarrel (the dogs I mean
Jonah and I were at a wedding
yesterday — all the way to London
It was a lovely time — starting

113

News about

the menfolk

finishing

the haymaking

but missing my help.

News about going

to a wedding,

about prizes

 for a show,

about Mr Batty's

car, "Jumbo"

falling to bits,

 about not

telling me what Jonah,

Old Fruit, said!

at 10 o'clock. Old fruit looked so smart in his best dark suit & white shirt - & cuffs showing below his jacket sleeves !!! My new hat looked very smart too - I didn't find a pair of blue shoes to tone with the dress and jacket - so had to make do with beige court - & handbag and gloves to match. It was a very nice wedding and a good reception - wine flowing like water - Jonah said it was good, but I didn't have any. We were home about 5.30 - and down to work again with a bump - Jonah off to the farm - and me is preparing puddings for dinner

during the afternoon 7 new visitors had arrived. Betty dishoned imagine had a busy day. The next exciting thing is the show on Thursday - a Harvest Festival on a dinner plate I wonder how we shall manage that! Friday Never had a minute to finish your letter and now the show is over - Betty looked the second prize with the Harvest on a dinner plate and I managed the Autumn berries etc - 1st prize and a special for the best arrangement in the flower classes. Betty's prize was 5/- and mine 7/6 and 10/- Think we'll back a HORSE !! Mr Batty has just bought another car - he almost lost the

petrol tank from his old car it had rusted away and finally dropped off at one side while driving through Loweswater - so that is the end of JUMBO as he called it - the other one arrived today Morris 1100 - white with red inside - 3 years old I think - it looks very nice - he cannot manage it very well just yet bumped a car standing in the front of the house tonight - I dare not tell you what Old fruit said !! I don't think it would be wise !!! Bedtime now so I'll finish and pop off to bed - Jonah and Betty have already gone - we all seem

As I began to return, I felt a sense of liberation from only being in Buttermere with the burden of sadness and loss. I began to see the beauty or smell the freshness or hear the calls of animals and birds or hear and feel the movement of water and weather. I could photograph the beauty. I travelled at Dawn and Dusk and if a new sadness came I went to take comfort once more. Thankful for my senses and for being alive.

I still do.

Goodbye Hello

I travelled at dawn
entering
the shrouded valley
to say goodbye.
Delicate mists
on the tops
of mountains.
As if commanded
Barn owl flew
alongside me
a swirling swooping
white winged beauty
which took my breath away.
Rare red squirrel
tearing
in front of me to cross the road
at the very last moment.
Munching ewes
a welcome committee at my special spot.
I sat by the remains
of a tree ...
And you said hello

Claire

Autumn colours looking West across
Buttermere lake

Sunset over
Buttermere
lake
towards
Mellbreak

The grey
beach
through
the trees
where the
rowing
boats
were
once
moored

Buttermere
beauty

Haystacks in
the background

Dawn at

Dale Head

Sour Milk Ghyll

innocently cascading today
after creating two lakes in
a valley where there was
just one lake and creating
the fertile fields there now

Towards Comb beck

Sun through the mountain gap ... Great Gable peering at the famous Buttermere pines

The Buttermere pines
Claire

Classic
Crummock

Wood House Island on a Spring morning

Comb Beck - just a small hint of a white line through the Birch trees but tumbling loud enough to be heard all the way across Buttermere lake

Evening
light at
sunset's
end

127

There were many places to stay in the valley in previous centuries.

Gatesgarth Farm where my Father first stayed

Buttermere Hotel now the Youth Hostel

130

The Edmondson family once ran this hotel as well as The Fish Hotel

Edmondson's Buttermere Hotel, via Cockermouth

Abraham's Series, Keswick

COACHES ARRIVING AT BUTTERMERE.

Adventurers
arrivals and
departures

Now Buttermere Court Hotel since the last Buttermere publicans, part of the Richardson, family left

Royal
Victoria
Hotel now
The Bridge
Hotel

Royal Victoria Hotel, Buttermere

No. 1265

J. L. Topaz Production

E 724   BALCONY BEDROOM. VICTORIA HOTEL. BUTTERMERE   BANKEYS.

Syke House Farm

J. 1. SYKE HOUSE. BUTTERMERE.

Table awaits at Syke House Farm

138

Hassness

Now staying at Wood House on my seven day return, I was finally ready to make an early morning visit to Scale Force.
Usually the path there was always wet. It had been dry for days.
I had told Tony Mckenzie I was going off at dawn.
" Yes just an hour there and back" he said with a slight smile

I didn't need the alarm clock I didn't use my head banging pillow bashing technique. I woke before dawn. It was all the more exciting because I had to be absolutely quiet... didn't want to wake the guests. This was in spite of the en-suite distancing me from Room 2, as it never had in Annie's days. Then, there was only one bathroom and a separate one toilet for us all.

My backpack contained everything I could possibly need. My Father's adopted motto for survival has rung in my ears for my whole life ... be prepared. I crept down the main staircase, picked up my walking boots, opened the front door with the knack of fifty years and stepped outside.

The sunlight was just entering the valley and mists hovered around the lakes, reeds and trees. I strode out to Buttermere village. Only a solitary crow's call with a distant echo from the fells accompanied me. A waking blackbird took its place. This sweetest of songs I imagined as a herald just for me. I was filled with the sensation of a return to patterned tides.

The hour that this walk would take, as predicted by Tony, I knew would be far more. I literally dawdled in solitary wonder. The beauty before me. Totally alone. Not a living soul to see me.

Buttermere was mine.

I took photo after photo and all the while I was incredulous to be so alone.

I went past the Fish Hotel over Scale bridge with the long trailing underwater weeds waving and undulating as they always had.

The greys, violets, blues of dawn and subtly changing mists lifted and all began to be illuminated by the sun's rays

as I walked on the path to Scale Force.

A solitary Heron was a temporary

escort

Mists hovered over Crummock Water with Hen House Wood trees in the background and Rannerdale beyond.

Sunlight
   on the fell tops
above Scale Bridge

Views glancing back to the head of the valley

144

Sunlit colours to warm the heart

Reflections towards the valley entrance in the North

Scale Force is hidden to the left of Crummock Water's edge

Scale Force appears at last

147

Scale Force

9 June 2019

Part of a letter home that I wrote
right by Scale Force [S.F.]
on Annie's birthday!

Guess where I am writing this from? NO - at Scale Force. We took the boat across to S.F. Beck and followed the Beck up to S.F. I have never seen it before and it is the most marvellous experience.

The waterfall has gouged out a deep chanel up which gusts of wind blow the spray.

David and I climb up as far as we could - the water falls really quickly.

Waterfall

Cascades of
mountain water tumbling down
Clear
crisp
dampness
deep in a cavernous gorge
where the air is bound with spray.
Here fronded ferns survive
Catching
lonely shafts
of sunlight
reflected on a patchwork moss carpet
lacy leaves
bowed
with droplets.
Listen to the waterfall's magic music
see the
glistening
dragonflies
born of water with iridescent wings.
Taste
the rich
cleansing
water
sit in timeless admiration

Claire April 1981

Scale Force by Sarah Annie Burns aged 16

As I made my way back to the waterfall
I could hear the echoes of voices

"What a bog. Never go there" Jonah calling in fun to me
and Annie singing of the joys to be found.
Father showing me how to see and describe beauty
and Mother teaching me how to hold on.
Brother David giving me a love of story
and photography.
Peter my brother ... a shadow throughout the journey.

   Here I was just myself

I almost couldn't wait to get as close as I could
to the falling water. I stood straight, balanced
on the rocks beneath.

Without a thought I suddenly shouted louder
than I had ever shouted for you all,
I love you I love you I love you.
I no longer was going to cry at the
inevitable shutting of the gate.
I had opened it myself.

In remembrance of

Peter Martin Griffel
Wladimir Griffel
Sarah Annie Burns
Jonah Robinson Todhunter
Dorothy Griffel nee Hodson